The Weather

RAIN

Terry Jennings

Chrysalis Children's Books

First published in the UK in 2004 by

Chrysalis Children's Books

An imprint of Chrysalis Books Group PLC

The Chrysalis Building, Bramley Road, London W10 6SP

ISBN 1 84458 068 7

British Library Cataloguing in Publication Data for this book is available from the British Library.

Produced by Bender Richardson White

Editorial Manager: Joyce Bentley
Project Editor: Lionel Bender and Clare Lewis
Designer: Ben White
Production: Kim Richardson
Picture Researcher: Cathy Stastny
Cover Make-up: Mike Pilley, Radius

Printed in China

10 9 8 7 6 5 4 3 2 1

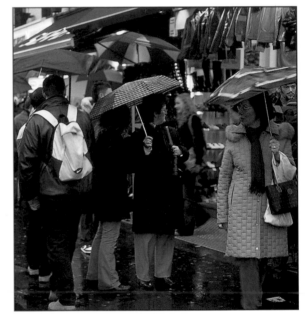

Words in **bold** can be found in New words on page 31.

Picture credits and copyrights
Corbis Images Inc.: cover (John M. Roberts) and pages 1, 17, 20, 23. Digital Vision Inc.: pages 13, 26. Ecoscene: pages 10 (Mike Whittle), 15 (Christine Osborne), 19 (Peter Currell), 27 (Pearl Bucknell). Lionheart Books: page 4. PhotoDisc Inc.: pages 22 (Adalberto Rios Szalay/Sexto Sol), 24 (Joseph Green/Life File), 28 (Adalberto Rios Szalay/Sexto Sol). Rex Features Ltd.: page 9 (Sipa). Steve Gorton: pages 2, 5, 6, 8, 11, 12, 18. Terry Jennings: pages 14, 16, 21, 25, 29. Weatherstock: page 5.

Contents

What is rain?

Rain is drops of water from the sky. When big raindrops fall hard, we say it is pouring with rain.

Sometimes the raindrops are small. Then we say it is **drizzling**. Raindrops collect on leaves and form **puddles**.

Rain from clouds

Rain is made when tiny drops of water inside **clouds** join together and get bigger.

Clouds get darker and darker. When the drops become too heavy to float, they fall as rain.

Getting wet

Rain can make you wet and uncomfortable. In wet weather, we wear clothes to keep our body dry.

We can also carry umbrellas to stop us getting wet.

Houses and rain

Houses have to keep out the rain. The roof and walls are **waterproof**.

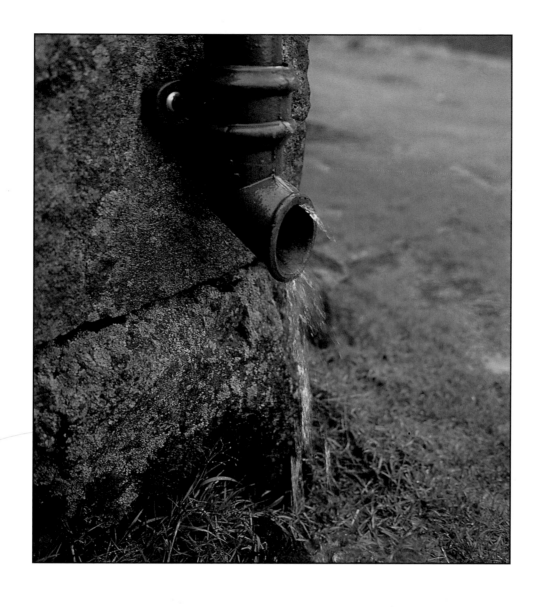

Special pipes, called **gutters** and **drainpipes**, carry the water away from the roof to the **drains**.

Rain fills rivers

Some of the rain that falls on hills and mountains flows down as **streams**.

Some streams make small waterfalls. As more rain fills streams, they grow into rivers.

Drinking water

Sometimes a big wall, called a **dam**, is built across a river. This makes a lake from which we get drinking water.

Some people get their drinking water from deep below the ground, at a **well**.

Lakes and ponds

These cows are drinking
from a **lake**. The lake
water came from rain.

These zebra in Africa are drinking from a **pond** called a waterhole. That water, too, came from rain.

Birds and rain

Water birds like rain. They do not get wet because their feathers are covered with oil from their bodies.

Other birds wash in garden
birdbaths when it rains.

Rain and plants

All plants need water if they are to grow. The plant roots take water from the soil. That water comes from rain.

These plants are dying
because it has not rained
and the soil is dry.

Rainforests

In some hot countries it rains nearly every day. Huge forests, called rainforests, grow in these places.

Many beautiful plants and
animals live in rainforests.

Deserts

Some places have little or no rain. The ground is nearly always very dry. These places are called **deserts**.

Where there is water in deserts, plants like these young **palm trees** grow.

Floods

Sometimes it rains so much that the rivers become too full. Then there is a **flood**.

Floods wash away soil and can damage houses, farms and cars.

Rainbows

Rainbows are bands of colours in the sky. They are made when the sun shines through raindrops.

The raindrops break up the white sunlight into seven different colours.

Quiz

1 Where does rain come from?

2 What kinds of clothes do we wear when it is raining?

3 What do streams grow into as they fill with rain?

4 What is the name of the big wall that is built across some rivers?

5 How do plants take water from the soil?

6 What do we call a place where hardly any rain falls?

7 What happens when rivers get too full of water?

8 How many colours are there in a rainbow?

The answers are all in this book!

New words

cloud a mass of tiny water drops floating in the air.

dam a wall built across a river to hold back water.

desert a large area of dry land.

drain a pipe or ditch for taking away rain or waste water.

drainpipe a tube for taking away water usually from a roof.

drizzling raining very tiny drops of water.

flood water from a river spreading over dry land.

gutter a channel along the edge of a roof to carry away rainwater.

lake a large area of water with land all around it.

palm tree a kind of tree with very large leaves that grows in hot countries.

pond a small area of water with land all around it.

puddle a pool of water on the ground.

stream a trickle of water flowing downhill; it joins with other streams to make a river.

waterproof keeps out water so things or people stay dry.

well a hole in the ground from which water is collected.

Index